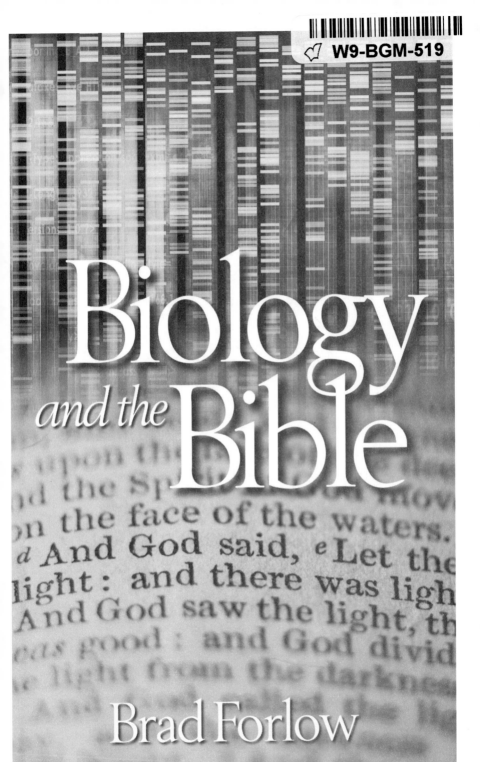

Biology
and the Bible

Brad Forlow

Biology
and the Bible

Brad Forlow

INSTITUTE FOR
CREATION
RESEARCH

Dallas, Texas
www.icr.org

BIOLOGY AND THE BIBLE

by Brad Forlow, Ph.D.

All Scripture quotations are from the New King James Version.

ISBN: 978-1-935587-14-9

Please visit our website for other books and resources: www.icr.org

Printed in the United States of America.

TABLE OF CONTENTS

INTRODUCTION

Most of us were budding biologists as children, exploring the world around us to satisfy our curiosity about the plants and animals and insects we observed. Often we would wonder about how birds could fly or how fish could hold their breath or how a tadpole could become a frog. And in school, we were able to peer through the lens of a microscope to see the tiniest of life swimming about underneath the surface of the ordinary.

Biology, of course, simply means "the study of life," and as adults, we know that life is much more complex than what we imagined as children.

And while many of us did not find a career in biology, we still marvel at the many expressions of life around us. As adults, we consider important questions about life. How did life begin? What makes humans distinct from animals? Is there any truth to the theories promoted by Charles Darwin and other evolutionists?

As Christians, we also want to know how the origin of life is described in the Bible. Did God really create all things in just six days? Were Adam and Eve real people or just symbols of human life? Or were they simply products of biological change from primates to humans?

Darwin's expedition on the *HMS Beagle* led him to the Galapagos Islands where he conducted research on the much publicized finches. The results of his study were instrumental in his writing of the now famous book *The Origin of the Species*, which has impacted the study of biology for over 150 years.

For many scientists and educators, biology and evolution are inseparable, and the study of biology remains at the forefront of the battle between biblical creation and evolutionary theory. Many today doubt or reject God's Word because they feel it is at odds with the "truth" of Darwinian evolution.

Are you confused about how to reconcile your beliefs with what is reported on the news or what is now being taught as authoritative truth in schools and universities, even in Christian schools?

Has your faith and the validity of God's Word been challenged by questions related to biology? Maybe you wrestle with questions such as these:

- How do we explain the tremendous diversity and variation displayed in creation?
- Have we evolved from apes, or are humans unique creations?
- Can mutations be beneficial for biological development?
- Was death a part of God's perfect creation?
- How did so many people groups arise from Adam and Eve?
- Were Adam and Eve really the first human couple?
- Have new scientific discoveries "proven" that Darwin's theories are true?

Believing that the Bible is the divinely inspired, inerrant, and authoritative Word of God, we trust it for answers to the questions of life, including biology. Therefore, we first look to God's Word to address the issue of biological origins.

In fact, biology cannot be rightly studied if the Bible is not taken seriously. Two events recorded in Genesis changed the world and impacted every discipline of science—the Curse of mankind, including all of creation, and the global Flood. Have you ever considered the significant impact that these events had on biology?

The biblical account of creation and the evolutionary approach to science proclaim mutually exclusive worldviews regarding biological origins and other aspects of biology. Many call into question the validity of God's Word based on evolutionary ideas that have permeated the study of biology and biological origins.

This book is designed to equip you with answers to prevalent questions about biology and the Bible, and to make you aware of the theological compromises that result when one attempts to integrate evolutionary science into the Genesis record. The following chapters address various biological topics readily attacked by those trying to undermine the authority of God's Word. Not surprisingly, the biblical account continues to be confirmed by new scientific discoveries.

By the end of your study, you should be confident in using God's Word to address issues in biology, including biological origins, as you encounter those who are determined to dismiss the biblical message in favor of evolution.

The Bible is not at odds with science. Rather, science confirms the text of Scripture and the very words of our Creator.

CHAPTER

GOD WHO GIVES LIFE

God, who gives life to the dead and calls those things which do not exist as though they did. (Romans 4:17)

Who am I? Why am I here? Where did I come from? What is my purpose in life? And let's not forget the one elusive question that everyone still asks—*Which came first, the chicken or the egg?* These questions have resonated throughout history. And they all point to the fundamental question: What is life and how did it begin?

How do you answer questions about our biological origins? Are these issues of faith, science, or both? Is the Bible right, or is science right? And while the Bible is not a science textbook, can you find answers to the questions of life, including biological origins, in the pages of Scripture?

For many, just the mention of biology may conjure up images of students dissecting frogs in a high school lab permeated with the smell of formaldehyde. Biology is the study of life and living organisms, including their origins. But where, when, and how did it all begin?

As Christians, we should be compelled to find answers to the questions of life in God's Word. After all, Genesis, the foundation of the Christian message in the Bible, means "origin." So, it shouldn't be surprising that within the book of Genesis we find clear answers to the origins of biological life.

The opening pages of Genesis tell us that God created everything out of nothing. Only God can create like that. God spoke, and things came into being. Because God is the only eternal, self-existing being, all life derived from Him. He is the source of all living things, and all things are dependent upon Him. God is now the conserver and preserver of life, for "in Him we live and move and have our being" (see Acts 17:23-31, Nehemiah 9:6, Hebrews 1:3). Life on earth is not merely an accident.

The earth was fashioned to be inhabited (Isaiah 45:18). And in just six days, God created, formed, and filled His creation (Genesis 1-2). He made the grasses (vegetation), plants (shrubs, herbs), fruit trees (Genesis 1:11), creatures in the water (Genesis 1:20), birds to fill the skies (Genesis 1:20), land creatures (cattle, creeping things, and beasts of the earth) to populate the planet (Genesis 1:24), and, ultimately, He breathed life into the specially-made creature called man (Genesis 2:7). All things, including biological life, were brought into existence by a supernatural act of God. When we consider the intricate details and the sophisticated design of all creation, we see that creation reveals the Creator—God is the source of biology.

All things, including biological life, were brought into existence by a supernatural act of God.

What about the claims of evolutionary science? Where does evolution fit with biological origins? Most of us have been exposed to the theory of evolution throughout our entire lives, in science and history classes, books and movies, and current events and news stories. Does evolution explain the creation account in Genesis, perhaps telling us *how* God created? Could evolution clarify the details of creation?

The theory of evolution as it relates to biological origins was popularized by Charles Darwin over 150 years ago. According to the theory, more complex and advanced species developed over the course of millions of years through slow and gradual changes brought about by random genetic mutations, natural selection, and survival of the fittest. This means that all species could be traced back to a single common ancestor, illustrated by the evolutionary "tree of life." But what does this type of biological progress require? At some point in the distant past, life had to develop from non-life.

Hasn't science proven that life can develop from non-life (i.e., organic, non-living materials), supporting the claims of evolutionary science?

Perhaps you recall studying about the Miller-Urey experiment that sought to prove life could have spontaneously arisen from some sort of primordial soup of complex chemicals (i.e., abiogenesis). In the experiment, an "atmosphere" of hydrogen, water vapor, methane, and ammonia were exposed to electrical discharges (simulating lightning) to form amino acids.

But can the formation of amino acids, the building blocks of proteins, be extrapolated as proof that life can arise from non-life? What about the formation of proteins, cells, and organs? Could this really occur spontaneously from a mixture of chemicals?

The conclusion drawn from this experiment crumbles under scientific scrutiny. First, the experiment excluded the presence of oxygen, claiming the atmosphere lacked oxygen at the time of biological origins. However, new data indicate that the earth has always been an oxygen-rich environment with conditions that would have destroyed the created amino acids. Second, biological systems are designed to only produce and utilize left-handed amino acids to make proteins, but the amino acids formed from the non-living system occurred in both right-handed and left-handed forms. The occurrence of the wrong orientation indicates that they are not the type of amino acids found in living things. Third, the energy provided by electrodes and required to form the amino acids would have destroyed proteins in the primitive atmosphere. Fourth, even though amino acids were formed, no mechanism existed to produce proteins.[1]

Is it rational to assume that living systems spontaneously form from non-living chemicals? The complexity of genetic systems and the intricacy of cellular processes are nearly impossible to comprehend. The formation of just one cell is infinitely more complex than the formation of simple amino acids. Yet, to explain biological origins in purely natu-

The complexity of genetic systems and the intricacy of cellular processes are nearly impossible to comprehend.

ralistic terms, the evolutionist must assume atmospheric conditions that did not exist in the past and processes that do not occur today to generate primitive organisms that no longer exist.[2]

Interesting ideas, but not science.

Unfortunately, even though evolution is not supported by empirical (testable) scientific data or evidence, it is nonetheless presented as true science and taught in our schools, colleges, universities, and even in our churches.

However, Darwin devised evolution as a naturalistic mechanism to explain biological origins apart from God, denying a supernatural creation. Evolutionary science is rooted in an atheistic and naturalistic worldview that rejects a need for God as the divine Creator, discredits the Bible as an authoritative source of truth, and disregards the gospel message, casting doubt on any intelligent purpose in creation.

Thus, the theory of evolution does not help us understand the meaning of the Genesis creation account, nor does it provide a feasible explanation of biological origins. The biblical message and evolutionary theory are mutually exclusive worldviews.

Life cannot come from non-life. Life can only come from God, who is life (John 5:26). Look to God who gives life for answers to the questions of life, including biological origins (John 1:1-4, Romans 4:17, 1 Timothy 6:13). Biological life is the handiwork of an intelligent, all-powerful Creator whom we should humbly worship in awe. God is the Author of life and the origin of all biological organisms.

ACCORDING TO ITS KIND

Then God said, "Let the earth bring forth the living creature according to its kind: cattle and creeping thing and beast of the earth, each according to its kind"; and it was so. And God made the beast of the earth according to its kind, cattle according to its kind, and everything that creeps on the earth according to its kind. (Genesis 1:24-25)

Have you ever been to a large zoo with a group of kids? If so, chances are good that you were pulled in many different directions, with each child clamoring to see a favorite animal. You probably found yourself surrounded by little voices, pleading their cases—*I want to see the elephants and giraffes. Let's go to the bird show. Can we see the penguins now? The monkeys are this way. Where are the lions and tigers?* They make sure you don't miss the rhinos, hippos, and bears. And someone actually wants to the visit the serpentarium—the house that exhibits lizards, snakes, and alligators. Our field trip gives us a glimpse into the astounding diversity of animals that inhabit the earth beyond the enclosures of the zoo.

Life in the ocean ranges from microscopic plankton to whales that weigh a ton. The ocean holds tiny shrimp, colorful tropical fish, eels, octopuses, dolphins, and great white sharks. Pelicans, parrots, owls, bats, hawks, eagles, and vultures soar through the skies. Spiders, lizards, squirrels, otters, coyotes, horses, mountain lions, deer, bears, and bison inhabit the lands around us.

In the 1700s, his realization of the great diversity displayed in creation led scientist Carolus Linnaeus to classify and describe various species of animals and plants. His work laid the foundation for the classification system that scientists use today for identifying and grouping distinctive kinds of biological organisms according to kingdom, phylum, class, order, family, genus, and species. What drove Linnaeus to begin classifying biological organisms? He was attempting to define biblical kinds—how biological organisms are classified in the Genesis creation account.

God Created Different Kinds

We can learn some important points from the biblical text about biological origins. In Genesis, we find that God created different "kinds" of biological organisms. Mature grasses (ground-covering vegetation), herbs (plants, bushes, shrubs), and fruit trees were all created to yield seed *according to their kinds* (Genesis 1:11-13). Likewise, living creatures in the waters, birds in the skies, and living creatures on land were all created to reproduce *according to their kinds* (Genesis 1:20-25). Each "kind" (Hebrew, *min*) was created to multiply or reproduce according to that type of organism.

But what does biblical "kind" correspond to in today's classification system? Linnaeus defined a species as a group of organisms (of the same type) that could interbreed among themselves to produce offspring of the same type. Does this sound familiar? Because this definition is similar to the principle of the biblical kind, many assume kind is equivalent to species. However, equating biblical kinds exclusively with species is too narrowly focused.

For instance, lions and tigers are classified as different species. But lions and tigers can actually breed to produce a *liger*. This suggests that lions and tigers both were produced from a more generalized "cat kind" from which various species of cats developed. Likewise, horses and zebras can interbreed to produce *zorses*, showing that both potentially stem from an initial "equine kind." Therefore, the biblical kind can be represented by species, genus, or family, depending on the specific example.[3]

> *"Kind" is used as a biological classification, referring to distinctive types of organisms.*

What, then, is meant by "kind" in God's creation?

"Kind" is used as a biological classification, referring to distinctive types of organisms. Each kind is separate from the other kinds. Biological living things were created fully formed and fully functional. The distinctive kinds of biological organisms have existed from the beginning, e.g., dogs have always been dogs, and fish have always been fish (1 Corinthians 15:38-39, James 3:12).

Scientific Insight

Evolution claims that all life has descended from a single common ancestor through the naturalistic processes of random mutations, natural selection, and survival of the fittest over millions of years. In opposition to what the Bible predicts, evolution asserts that the pattern of life is continuous. Based on this theory, all of life is genetically interrelated, the foundational premise to the famed "tree of life."

However, the creation account teaches us that the pattern of life is *discontinuous.*

So, what does science support—a discontinuous or continuous pattern of life? New scientific studies are shedding light on the classification of organisms and their relatedness. The comparison of genetic similarities between humans and other species is often invoked in favor of evolutionary development. Has science proven the hierarchal development of species (i.e., the tree of life and common ancestry) as evolution claims?

Consider these facts: A protein sequence comparison shows that pandas are 79 percent identical to humans. Tortoises are 75 percent, sea urchins are 60 percent, beetles are 59 percent, and yeast is 50 percent identical to humans.

Does this "hierarchy" in similarity prove descent from a common ancestor? Not when all the data are considered.

What would scientists expect when comparing sequences between two creatures that are supposedly more closely related to each other? For instance, what percent similarity would be expected between more closely related species like the beetle and yeast? If "simple" became more complex through evolutionary development, shouldn't the beetle (a simpler creature) be more closely related to yeast and show more similarity than when they

15

are compared to humans (a much more complex creature)?

Interestingly, when yeast is compared to all the other species, the percent of similarity is 50 percent for each comparison. This is not the expected result based on a continuous pattern of life as evolution predicts.

When compared between species, it appears that the yeast proteins are isolated, separate, and completely distinct from all other species. The yeast proteins cannot be arranged in any sort of hierarchy with other creatures. According to the data, yeast is no more related to the beetle than to a human.[4]

Evolutionists claim continuity between species because of their belief in descent from a common ancestor. But rather than verifying molecular continuity, the scientific data actually show discontinuity between species. Thus, the robust diversity of biological creatures is not due to natural selection or chance random mutations, rather, it is due to the perfect design of God who supernaturally created distinct kinds of plants and animals over six days about 6,000 years ago. With the creation of distinct kinds, biological discontinuity between different types of organisms is just what Genesis predicts.

> *The robust diversity of biological creatures is not due to natural selection or chance random mutations, rather, it is due to the perfect design of God.*

CHAPTER

BE FRUITFUL AND MULTIPLY
AND FILL THE EARTH

And God blessed them, saying, "Be fruitful and multiply, and fill the waters in the seas, and let birds multiply on the earth." (Genesis 1:22)

Have you ever walked through a botanical garden and been amazed by the numerous varieties of roses? Do you prefer Braeburn, Fuji, Gala, Golden Delicious, Granny Smith, McIntosh, Honeycrisp, or Jonathan apples? These are just a few of the over 7,500 varieties of apples worldwide. Window shopping for a new puppy at a local pet store may leave you struggling to decide between a Chihuahua, terrier, schnauzer, retriever, hound, spaniel, bulldog, or poodle. For the cat person, the choices are no less complicated—do you want a solid-colored, multi-colored, striped, or spotted cat? There are cats with big ears, small ears, long tails, no tails, short hair, medium hair, long hair, fluffy hair—and cats that have no hair and cats that look like rats.

Oh, the variety of God's creation! The vastness of creation includes an expansive array of biological variation within each kind of plant and animal.

Did you realize the enormous diversity and variation that we observe today cause many to question the validity of the biblical account? Critics argue that the magnitude of biological diversity and variation in the world is enormous. Over 1.5 million species of plants, animals, and other biological organisms have been described. However, some estimate that there could be upwards of 50-100 million unidentified and unnamed species,[5] and they use those inflated numbers to make a case for evolution.

Are these extraordinary numbers compatible with the biblical account of creation and the Flood? Did God create all these species during the creation week? If so, how would Adam have named them all in just one day? Could Noah have collected all of these species before the Flood? Could that many animals fit on the Ark? These are all questions raised by those who believe the "scientific evidence" discredits the Bible.

How would you answer critics that use the tremendous variety in God's creation as ammunition against the creation account and subsequently the account of the global Flood? Answering these questions requires an understanding of the term "biblical kind." Is the biblical "kind" equivalent to species? No. *Kind* doesn't equate to *species* in today's classification system of biological organisms.

All the species alive today were not created during creation week, as proponents of the fixity of species claim, so Adam did not have 1.5 million biological species to name. What did God instruct Adam to name? Every biological organism? Every species? Every kind? The Bible says that "every beast of the field and every bird" was brought to Adam and he gave names to all cattle, birds, and every beast of the field (Genesis 2:19-20). Most biblical creation scholars believe this to mean that Adam only named the created *kinds* of the types of animals specified.

Was Noah told to take every biological organism onto the Ark? No. Noah was only instructed to take certain animal *kinds*—not even every type of animal—"to keep seed alive upon the face of all the earth" (Genesis 6:19-21, 7:1-3, 8:17-19). This would have included mammals, birds, reptiles, and amphibians, as all air-breathing life was to be destroyed from the face of the earth (Genesis 6:13, 17). Even with a conservative estimate of 16,000 animals (based on equating the biblical kind with the modern genus), the Ark could have easily housed the animals in less than half of its capacity.[6]

Understanding terminology clears up any misunderstanding about Adam's naming of the animals and the Ark's ability to house the animals. Don't be confused about the Bible's creation account based on misapplied terminology.

But this leaves another point of contention for many. How can the vast biological variety (number of species) observed in our world be reconciled with the notion that everything has come from only those animals that were saved on the Ark? Is it feasible that all the bird and land animal species that exist today were produced in the relatively short period of time since the global Flood (rapid speciation)? Does scientific evidence support the rapid post-Flood speciation?

Evolutionary science would lead you to believe that it takes 100,000 to 10 million years for a new species to develop. But numerous examples exist that show biological organisms have rapidly changed within their kind to form new species. And it has been quite perplexing to evolutionists when new species have developed rapidly.[7] Can rapid speciation be explained scientifically? Yes. The explanation to rapid speciation lies within the complex interworking of the genetic code (DNA).

Scientific Insight

Our understanding of genetics provides valid scientific explanations for what is currently observed and what occurred following the Flood. The observable variation in an organism's appearance (the development of distinctively new physical characteristics) is largely based on the organism's genetic makeup.

The Flood changed the geological landscape of the earth. The Flood also had significant ramifications on biology. The newly altered environmental conditions after the Flood favored the rapid speciation of the animals exiting the Ark.

> *The Flood changed the geological landscape of the earth. The Flood also had significant ramifications on biology.*

What conditions promoted rapid speciation—the increased variation (of physical characteristics that produces new species) of the existing genetic material?

Small inbreeding populations of animals existed immediately after the Flood. These unique and genetically distinct descendants migrated around the globe, settled in the appropriate environments based on their genetic makeup, and became geographically and reproductively isolated. As they continued to reproduce, once two populations of animals possessing variations of some genes were completely separated, two species would result that differ in appearance (color, size, etc.) and behavior. Migration, segregation, and reproductive isolation lead to speciation, even rapid speciation under the right conditions.[8]

Can genetics alone account for the vast variety that is observed today? Absolutely!

The potential for genetic variation and subsequent speciation is extensive. Various sources cause changes in the genetic sequence of an organism, and variation results from alterations in the genetic material.

Variation can be caused by different gene DNA sequences (as in gene alleles or polymorphisms) within individuals. The genetic makeup of an individual is also governed by the inheritance of genes from the mother and father (homologous recombination). Chemical modification of DNA and differences in gene regulation are also sources of variation. Additional variation occurs through the mutation of genes.[9]

Regardless of the source of variation, the genetic material from which all variety arises was present from the start. Variation results from changes to *existing* genetic material. No new genetic material is created when variations occur (which would be required for an organism to change into a different kind). And contrary to the claims of evolutionists, even mutations do not create different kinds.

God created extensive biological diversity with a wide range of different plant and animal kinds. However, each biological kind was created with *genetic potential*—the amount of variation that a kind of organism can produce from the genetic material that is already present as it reproduces "according to its kind." This genetic design has resulted in a variety of specialized subgroups as descendants of each created kind continue to multiply and fill the different habitats and environmental niches of the earth in accordance with God's command following both creation and Noah's Flood.[10] Praise God for the diversity and variation of biological species that fill His magnificent creation.

IN THE IMAGE OF GOD

Then God said, "Let Us make man in Our image, according to Our likeness; let them have dominion over the fish of the sea, over the birds of the air, and over the cattle, over all the earth and over every creeping thing that creeps on the earth." So God created man in His own image; in the image of God He created him; male and female He created them.
(Genesis 1:26-27)

Do you ever marvel at the capacities of the human body? The eye can focus on the words of this page or on the snow atop a mountain a mile away. The human hand can delicately hold a fragile egg or grasp and lift a 50-pound bucket. The legs can walk, run, bike, or dance gracefully across the ground. The brain can recall an event that occurred many, many years ago or learn a new language. The tongue can distinguish between salty, sour, bitter, and sweet.

The human body is one of the most remarkable specimens in all of creation. Consider the intricate design and amazing complexity of your genetic, cellular, and organ systems.

Consider the intricate design and amazing complexity of your genetic, cellular, and organ systems.

Your genetic code (DNA composed of 3 billion nucleotides) is the set of instructions that encode tens of thousands of genes, specifying the characteristics that make you unique, such as your hair color, eye color, height, and blood type.

Your body is composed of 60 trillion cells (200 different types of cells, varying in size, shape, and function), and each carries out an average of 10 million chemical reactions per second.[11]

Your organs are precisely coordinated systems of cells and cellular networks. For example, the brain processes data faster than a supercomputer. Some processes related to your body's motion happen at about 2 million signals per second! The 16 billion neurons in the body can send messages between the brain and parts of the body at 300 miles per hour. The eye is constructed from numerous intricate components, including the lens, iris, cornea, pupil, retina, muscles, veins, and optic nerve. But what happens if you are missing the cornea, the iris, or the optic nerve? You wouldn't be able to see anything![12]

And what does this have to do with biological origins?

The eye, like many biological systems, is not just complex, it is "irreducibly complex." This is also referred to as all-or-nothing functionality. In other words, removing a single component prevents the entire system from working. All the parts of a system had to be in place and properly functioning from the beginning for the eye to work.[13]

This is in contrast to evolutionary science that contends that "simple" has evolved into "complex," slowly and gradually. But life is not simple. All of life is complex—from the information of the genetic code, to the processes of a single cell, to the finely tuned organs. Amazing complexity, intricate design, and the remarkable all-or-nothing functionality of our bodies reveal an all-powerful and all-knowing Creator.

Made in the Image of God

Our bodies provide a great example of the incomprehensible complexity and design of the Creator. But what sets humanity apart from the plants and animals? Are we just another higher ordered biological organism?

From the beginning, Adam and Eve were created distinct from the plant and animal kingdoms.

Not according to God. In Genesis, we are told not only of the origins of plants and animals, but also of humanity, the pinnacle of God's Creation.

God formed man (Adam) from the dust of the ground, and breathed into his nostrils the breath of life; and man became a living being (Genesis 2:7). When no helpmate was found for Adam from within the animal kingdom, the woman Eve was made from one of Adam's ribs (Genesis 2:18-22). From the beginning, Adam and Eve were created distinct from the plant and animal kingdoms. They were given authority *over* the animals as stewards of God's creation (Genesis 1:26-28, 2:15-17, 9:1-7; Mark 10:6). In Genesis, we find that both animals and humans have life, soul, and spirit. But Adam and Eve were created *in the image of God* (Genesis 1:26-27). No other part of creation is given this distinction.

Although humans and animals display many similarities in physiological makeup, the human body is still unique. Humans can also show a vast range of feelings and emotions, and there is an almost infinite variation of dispositions, behavioral tendencies, talents, abilities, tastes, interests, attitudes, and values. The intellect of humans immensely exceeds animals, including memory, reason, abstract thought, imagination, creativity, speech, song, and worship.

Evolution contends that humanity, the highest order of evolved species, is a product of chance. But the Genesis account tells a different story. The gap between animals and humans is unbridgeable, setting humanity apart from the animal kingdom and dismissing any notion of relatedness.

Scientific Insight

You are probably familiar with the image of a monkey morphing into a modern man. It has become synonymous with Darwinian evolution. Many critics of the biblical account point to science to uphold the claims of human-monkey ancestry.

How do you answer the critics that tout the human-chimpanzee genetic similarity studies as proof of human evolution and common ancestry? (Evolutionists claim that the DNA sequence is 98 percent identical, but creation scientists disagree with that percentage.) Has science shown that we are descendants of chimpanzees? Much has been made about these scientific claims. But is the correlation between DNA sequence similarity and human-chimpanzee relatedness even valid?

New data continue to wreak havoc on evolutionary claims of human-chimpanzee relatedness and the idea of common ancestry. Consider the following issues: First, the data are misleading and biased, based on the genetic segments chosen for comparison. Only human and chimp DNA sequence fragments that already exhibited a high level of similarity were selected for analysis. Second, subsections of the two genomes don't match, showing little, if any, similarity. There are actually large blocks of sequence anomalies that are not directly comparable and would yield a similarity of zero percent in some regions. Third, sequence similarity studies often compare the protein coding portions of genes while ignoring other parts, like gene regulation segments. However, most of DNA codes for gene regulation, not proteins. Therefore, some of the most critical DNA sequences are often omitted from sequence similarity comparisons.[14]

Although evolutionists continue to tout genetic sequence similarities, it is important to recognize that there is more to the story than just DNA sequence similarity. Many factors besides gene sequence explain the physiological and behavioral differences that show humans and chimpanzees were distinctly created. New scientific discoveries are showing that the differences in traits between organisms are more dependent upon *gene regulation*, not simply gene sequence.[15]

Evolution contends that humanity is a mere product of chance that occurred over millions of years of biological development. From the evolutionary viewpoint, there is no God. In addition, there is no purpose, no value, and no meaning to life. Those who adopt the evolutionary frame of reference often think that they get to choose their own destiny. Evolution has fostered a humanistic and naturalistic view of man in relation to the environment and animals, as many worship and serve the creature rather than the Creator (Romans 1:18-25).

The complex, intricate biological design of humanity stands against the claims of evolutionary science and points to a Creator. As descendants of Adam and Eve, you, too, have been created in the very image of God. You were formed by God. You are a unique, special creation, "fearfully and wonderfully made" (see Psalm 139:14, Jeremiah 1:5). Your life is valued by God. Your life has reason, purpose, and meaning—to worship God your Creator and live in relationship with Him (Luke 12:6-8).

CHAPTER

EVERY TRIBE AND TONGUE AND PEOPLE AND NATION

You are worthy to take the scroll, And to open its seals; For You were slain, And have redeemed us to God by Your blood Out of every tribe and tongue and people and nation, And have made us kings and priests to our God; And we shall reign on the earth. (Revelation 5:9-10)

D o you ever just sit and watch people—maybe at the airport, or in the mall, in the park, or at your favorite restaurant? Consider the diversity of individuals that you encounter on a daily basis. Did you know that there are more than 16,000 people groups living in the 195 nations that exist in the world today? Remarkably, over 6,500 languages and dialects are currently spoken throughout the world.[16]

Unfortunately, we live in a world with racial tension within and among the nations. However, the Bible never speaks of different "races" of people. The biblical divisions of people include tongues, families, nations, and lands. The term "race" is strictly an evolutionary concept used by Darwin and others.[17] Are you aware that the full title for Darwin's famous book is actually *On the Origin of Species by Means of Natural Selection, or The Preservation of Favoured Races in the Struggle for Life?*

> **The Bible never speaks of different "races" of people.**

There may be many ethnicities among people, but there is only one humanity. God "has made from one blood every nation of men" (see Acts 17:24-26).

How, then, do you explain the abundance of ethnic groups and languages spoken if everyone is a descendant of Adam and Eve (and subsequently Noah and his sons' families)?

God commanded those that left the Ark to "Be fruitful and multiply, and fill the earth" (see Genesis 9:1). But this command of God was soon ignored.

After the Flood, all the nations of the world were formed from the descendants of Noah (Genesis 10:32), but there was still just one language (Genesis 11:1, 6). How did all the nations, people groups, and languages come into existence after the Flood from the sons of Noah?

The Bible says that instead of spreading around the earth, the descendants of Noah blatantly rebelled against God and decided to settle in one place. They desired to make a name for themselves, so they built a city and a tower "whose top is in the heavens" (see Genesis 11:1-4)—the Tower of Babel.

What was the result of their efforts? God judged their disobedience, interrupting mankind's plans at the Tower of Babel by confusing their language and scattering them over the face of the earth (Genesis 11:4-9). By giving them different languages, the families were forced to separate and to begin the process of filling the earth (Genesis 10:5, 20, 23, 31).

Distinct nations, people groups, and languages today are the result of the original dispersion of languages and families at Babel. The origination of nations, languages, and ethnic diversity was a supernaturally imposed act of God. The Table of Nations in Genesis 10 represents the earliest known distinct nations that began to spread around the world. The three basic streams of nations and languages—Semitic, Japhetic (Indo-European), and Hamitic—are still recognized by biblical scholars today (Genesis 10:5, 20, 31).

Scientific Insight

How does evolutionary science explain the multitude of different ethnic groups and languages? One theory contended that each of the major "races" had evolved independently in several areas from a different ape-like people (i.e., by simultaneous evolution at a differential rate of evolution).[18] Isn't it rather far-fetched that apes all over the earth simultaneously turned into humans and created their own language?

The Bible provides a rational explanation for the development of ethnic groups, languages, and nations. But is it scientifically valid? The imposed language barriers between families would have kept them isolated as they were scattered, resulting in the genetic isolation of small inbreeding populations. This scenario ensures that low frequency alleles (once latent in large populations) would become prominent, generating the rapid development of the distinctive physical characteristics associated with each ethnicity.[19]

> *The Bible provides a rational explanation for the development of ethnic groups, languages, and nations.*

Thus, the various physical characteristics of ethnicities (skin color, etc.) can be much more readily explained by the biblical account. Although everyone is a descendant of Adam and Eve (and Noah and his family), ethnic groups arose from the "enforced segregation" imposed by God following the confusion of language, so that humanity would multiply and fill the earth as commanded (Genesis 1:28, 9:1).

Can all of humanity really be traced back to a single couple? The historicity of Adam and Eve is validated throughout the Bible and even by the testimony of Jesus (1 Chronicles 1:1; Matthew 19:3-6; Mark 10:5-9; Luke 3:38; Acts 17:24-29; Romans 5:12-19, 8-20; 1 Corinthians 11:8-12, 15:21-22, 45-47; 2 Corinthians 11:3; Ephesians 5:30-32; Colossians 3:10; 1 Timothy 2:13-15; James 5:9; Jude 1:14). Denying a literal Adam and Eve has significant theological ramifications, undermining biblical authority and subsequently dismissing original sin, the Fall, and the gospel message itself.

Those who reject a literal Adam and Eve even point to science in their defense, claiming that studies show that genetic variation indicates a starting population of around 10,000 people. This has fueled the argument that humanity can't be traced back to a single couple.[20]

But scientific studies have shown that 6.7 percent of the human genetic code has dissimilar pairs of genes that are connected to many recognizable traits (heterozygous allelic variation). Although the degree of difference in the genetic code might appear insignificant, calculations based on just 6.7 percent of dissimilar pairs of genes show that a human couple in theory could produce 10^{2017} distinct children before they would have a child identical to another.[21] The genetic code of one couple—Adam and Eve—has resulted in the tremendous ethnic diversity that exists all around the world today.

But doesn't the existence of Neanderthals prove evolutionary development? Neanderthal remains have been mostly found in European caves, but also in China. Genetic studies show DNA sequence similarity between Europeans and Neanderthals. Archaeological evidence and genetic comparisons corroborate that Neanderthals and modern-looking humans intermarried.[22]

We now know that the so-called "early man" was nothing more than a "real" human being, living in a simple and degenerate culture. The existence of "cavemen" actually fits the biblical account of post-Babel dispersion. With primitive conditions forced upon humankind for a time, it's reasonable to expect that humans existed as cavemen. And as people fled into the wilderness, moving away from Babel, they needed shelter, food, tools, and protection (Job 30:3-8).

Adam and Eve were the literal first couple of humanity. Neanderthals are not "archaic" people, but they are one group of the diverse population of people that migrated to fill the earth. Ethnic groups were originally established by God as He separated the people by language—every tribe, tongue, people, and nation can be traced back to God's judgment at the Tower of Babel.

But God's heart for the nations is evident all throughout Scripture—from the Abrahamic covenant, to the purpose of the nation of Israel, to the Great Commission, to the journeys of Paul and the other apostles, and to the picture given around the throne. Humanity, made up of every tribe, tongue, people, and nation, was created distinctly in the image and likeness of God. Humans were created to worship Him—now and in eternity (Revelation 5:8-10, 7:9-12).

CHAPTER

THORNS AND THISTLES

Cursed is the ground for your sake; In toil you shall eat of it All the days of your life. Both thorns and thistles it shall bring forth for you.
(Genesis 3:17-18)

For thousands of years, seekers have pursued the ever-elusive fountain of youth, the legendary spring of water that was sure to restore youth to those who drank from it. Many today try to stop or reverse the natural processes of biological decay, still in pursuit of the fountain of youth, but in different forms—creams, diets, gym memberships, spa treatments, and even surgeries.

Today, the oldest person in the world is reportedly 127 years old! Advances in medicine and technology have prolonged the lifespan of many, but even 127 years doesn't seem so impressive when you compare it to biblical lifespans.

What happened to the biblical days when people lived hundreds of years? Why are biological organisms and processes deteriorating, even to the point

What happened to the biblical days when people lived hundreds of years?

of extinction? Why is decay so evident in our lives and in our world? What happened to God's perfect creation?

As a result of Adam's sin, the serpent, woman, man, and all of creation were cursed (Genesis 1-3). Thorns and thistles began to epitomize the cursed ground (Romans 8:20-22, Hebrews 1:10-12, 1 Peter 1:24). Sorrow, pain, suffering, sweat, tears, and physical death now characterize life.

29

But how do we explain the presence of detrimental organisms in our world that couldn't have been considered part of the perfect creation? Although the biblical text doesn't specifically list these, we can extrapolate that various biological nemeses existing in our world today resulted from the Curse, including biological poisons, microbial pathogens, harmful bacteria, viruses, weeds, and parasites.[23] The Curse affected the biology of the whole world. All of creation "groans and labors with birth pangs until now" as the whole world is subject to the "bondage of corruption" (see Romans 8:21-22); "corruption" means "decay" in this passage, underscoring the ongoing effects of the Curse, even until today.

The global Flood was sent by God to destroy all life on earth as judgment for sin and wickedness in the world. The earth after the Flood was drastically different—geologically, meteorologically, and even biologically. Many of the changes in the "new" world (e.g., climate changes such as temperature extremes, storms, increased radiation, and the ice age) resulted in an environment that is hostile to life (Job 6:15-17, Genesis 13:10).

The earth after the Flood was drastically different— geologically, meteorologically, and even biologically.

What proof indicates that biological changes have occurred since the Flood? One evidence is found in the rocks and fossils that the Flood formed. Prior to the Flood, tropical conditions existed all around the world.[24] Plants and animals were much larger than they are today—dragonflies with 30-inch wingspans, enormous dinosaurs, and huge plants and trees. We have found within rocks the fossilized remains of numerous species that no longer exist.

Another evidence is recorded in Scripture. Many wonder about the lengthy lifespans of people in the Bible. Adam, Seth, Enos, Methuselah, and Noah all lived over 900 years. Noah's son, Shem, who was born before the Flood, lived 600 years. But the lifespan of people shortened rapidly after the Flood. Many lived to be over 450 years, including Arphaxad, Salah, and Eber. Genesis records that Peleg, Reu, and Serug lived approximately 230 years. Abraham, Isaac, and Jacob died at the ages of 175, 180, and 147 years, respectively. Joseph lived to be 110 years old. The expected lifespan around the time of Moses was about 70 years (Psalm 90:10), and today—depending on where you live—average lifespans are about the same.

Scientific Insight

Where did the thorns and thistles come from? How did biological nemeses originate? What happened to the very large plants and animals? Why did people in the Old Testament live so long? Why have human lifespans significantly declined since the Flood?

Scientists have developed many hypotheses to answer these questions. For instance, it is possible that thorns, thistles, and biological nemeses may have arisen through the "turning on" of latent genetic information. However, a prominent and logical scientific explanation for the biological degeneration due to the Curse is genetic decay caused by *mutations*.[25] Genetic mutations are a corruption of the perfect creation.

Mutations are changes in a gene's DNA sequence. Mutations can be inherited from parents or caused by copy errors when DNA replicates itself. DNA can also be damaged by environmental agents such as sunlight, cigarette smoke, viruses, mutagenic chemicals, and radiation.

Erroneously, the theory of evolution is based upon the speculation that mutations produce new and useful information that generates more complex structures, functions, and advanced species. However, this does not align with our knowledge and understanding of genetics and is completely opposite of what is observed scientifically.[26] Mutations do not add information or new genes.

Mutations occur to pre-existing material, damaging existing genes and resulting in a *loss* of information (and a loss of genetic potential). Most mutations produce little or no effect on the organism (neutral), but some are very harmful. Unfortunately, DNA mutations in an individual accumulate over time, referred to as *genetic burden* or *genetic load*. As the genetic burden increases, the survival of the species is threatened because offspring have a greater chance of being born with severe genetic defects.[27] If genetic mutations are advantageous, as evolutionary science claims, why does the body have elaborate DNA repair mechanisms that attempt to eliminate mutations?[28]

Some may ask, "But haven't certain beneficial mutations substantiated the evolutionary claims?" Many point to antibiotic resistance of bacteria or individual resistance to deadly diseases as proof of evolution through mutations. For instance, a certain mutation to hemoglobin results in individuals being resistant to malaria. Another mutation deleting a cell surface receptor leads to HIV resistance. Are these examples of evolutionary advancement through mutations? No! These individuals are rather serendipitously protected from certain pathogens. But scientific investigation shows that evolution did not occur in any of these situations. Mutations did not add genetic information that resulted in the advancement of a biological organism. In each case, there is actually a *loss* of information that renders the host less fit.[29]

Evolutionary advancement of biological organisms would require millions of innovative, helpful mutations that would add new information to the genetic code. This does not happen. Instead, we see a loss of information, the increase in disease, and finally extinction.

Biological systems and process are running down, species are going extinct, and we are all burdened with increasing health issues. Foundational to these biological issues is the cumulative effect of genetic mutations through the generations.

Many people today can rightly blame their health struggles on "bad genes." Medical practitioners rely heavily on family histories when they treat their patients because many diseases and disorders are linked to genetic mutations that are passed down through generations.

> *Many people today can rightly blame their health struggles on "bad genes."*

Mutations to DNA are harmful, causing sickness and even death. Mutations are often linked to various diseases. In fact, hundreds of human diseases and disorders are caused by a *single* gene defect, including Huntington's disease, polycystic kidney disease, sickle cell anemia, cystic fibrosis, and hemophilia.[30]

Although we live in a fallen world characterized by decay, disease, and death, we look forward to the day when God restores all things and makes all things new, including a new heaven and a new earth where disease, suffering, pain, and death are conquered (Colossians 1:15-23, 2 Peter 3:13, Revelation 21:4-5).

CHAPTER

TO DUST YOU SHALL RETURN

For out of it you were taken; For dust you are, And to dust you shall return. (Genesis 3:19)

If you ever watch *National Geographic* or *Animal Planet* programs, you might witness some gruesome images. Maybe you'll see the boa constrictor squeezing the life out of its dinner. Or maybe you'll watch the lion or cheetah chasing and taking down a gazelle.

The "food chain" seems to be a natural part of our world. You know how the story goes: Grass provides food for the grasshopper, which gets eaten by a frog that becomes lunch for a snake, which is carried off for dinner by a hawk.

Not many things are certain in life, but one thing is guaranteed—death. Physical death is a natural part of life, a process of deterioration and decomposition. Cells lose structural integrity and cellular enzymes destroy surrounding tissues. Chemical processes cause the breakdown of proteins, carbohydrates, lipids, nucleic acids, and bone. Death results in a continuous loss of biological order and information that culminates in the triumph of chemistry over biology as the once living body returns to the dust from which it was made (Genesis 3:19).[31]

Many point to the natural order today (e.g., food chain) in an attempt to disprove the notion of a perfect creation that did not include death. If God, who is life, created a perfect world, then why is there biological death? How do we reconcile this dog-eat-cat-eat-rat world with the Genesis account of a perfect creation? Has our acceptance of death as a fact of life dispelled the notion of a perfect creation—one that did not contain death, not even the death of animals?

Biological development according to the evolutionary science paradigm is founded upon death. Death is a creative force necessary for biological advancement through random mutation, natural selection, and survival of the fittest. Ultimately, millions of years of death brought about the development of humans.

Is this consistent with the message of God's Word? Did physical death bring about man, or did man bring about physical death?

The Curse, pronounced upon creation as judgment for sin, introduced a plethora of biological changes into the world, most notably, the origin of physical death (Genesis 3:19). The idea of death before sin is in complete opposition to God's Word. It was Adam's sin that brought death into the world. Death is the penalty and punishment for sin (Romans 5:12, 6:23; 1 Corinthians 15:21-22). God's creation was perfect and did not include death. God is Life, not the author of death (John 1:1-4). Death is not a creative force of nature, but the last enemy of all things (1 Corinthians 15:26, Hebrews 2:14). Death was an intruder into the perfect world and will be conquered by Jesus (Revelation 21:4-5).

> *The Curse, pronounced upon creation as judgment for sin, introduced a plethora of biological changes into the world, most notably, the origin of physical death (Genesis 3:19).*

What happens to the natural order of life if we contend that there was no death before Adam's sin? How do we explain the food chain? Based on Scripture, this is easily reconciled. Just because it is happening now, doesn't mean it was happening then. In Genesis, we are told that there was no predation, no food chain, in God's "good" creation.

If God did not create a world with a food chain, what did everything eat? How did everything survive? Plants! Although not very appetizing to those who love a good hamburger or steak, plants were created to be a continually replenishing food source for both man and animals (Genesis 1:29-30).[32]

The Bible does not explicitly say when carnivorous activity began in the animal kingdom. This probably occurred sometime after the Curse as evil and violence in the world increased. However, people were not given permission to eat animals until after the Flood, when Noah was told that every moving thing that lives shall be food (Genesis 9:1-3).

Biblical "Life"

However, this leads to a further objection. Since both man and animals ate plants, doesn't that constitute death in the perfect world? To answer this question it is necessary to understand how the Bible defines life. What distinguishes the creation of plants, animals, and humans?

Plants are highly complex biological systems, composed of the same basic building blocks of life (DNA and cells) as animals and humans. But numerous aspects of plant life differ from animal and human life. Plants were "brought forth" from the earth, being formed from the dust of the earth. Animals and humans were "created," a term applied to both animals and humans, but not to plants. Plants do not possess a living soul as do animals and humans. Based on the terminology used in Genesis, plants do not have "life," a "soul," a "spirit," or "blood." However, all these terms are used to describe the creation of animal and human life.

Although plants grow and flourish, the Bible doesn't refer to plants as "living." They are biologically alive, but *not* biblically living. Since plants do not have biblical life, they do not "die" in the way that humans and animals die. Instead, they "wither" or "fade." A similar argument can be made for some of the "lower" animals (perhaps some types of worms, sponges, etc.), and certainly for protozoans and viruses. Their "death" would not constitute death of truly living organisms.[33]

> *Based on God's Word, we can confidently say that death did not exist in God's perfect creation, even in the animal kingdom.*

Is death a creative force that brought about biological advancement, or is death the consequence of man's sin? Based on God's Word, we can confidently say that death did not exist in God's perfect creation, even in the animal kingdom. God's Word emphatically states that man's sin brought physical (and spiritual) death into the world (Ephesians 2:5; Colossians 2:13,

3:3). This is the essence of the gospel. Jesus the Creator became the Savior to bring redemption of sin through His own death on the cross in order to bring us life and save us from death—both physical and spiritual (John 3:16, 5:26, 11:25, 14:6). John MacArthur stresses the importance of a proper understanding of Genesis 3 as the foundation for the rest of Scripture:

> Genesis 3 is one of the most vitally important chapters in all the Bible. It is the foundation of everything that comes after it. Without it, little else in Scripture or in life itself would make sense. Genesis 3 explains the condition of the universe and the state of humanity. It explains why the world has so many problems. It explains the human dilemma. It explains why we need a Savior. And it explains what God is doing in history.[34]

Incorporating death into God's perfect creation is inconsistent with God's nature, God's Word, and the gospel message. Yes, we live in a world characterized by a natural order that includes predation and death for survival. But we live in a fallen and cursed world. Do not interpret Scripture through the lens of nature. Instead, interpret nature through the authority of God's Word.

CHAPTER

LIFE IN THE BLOOD

For the life of the flesh is in the blood, and I have given it to you upon the altar to make atonement for your souls; for it is the blood that makes atonement for the soul. (Leviticus 17:11)

The cardiovascular system includes the heart, blood vessels, and blood. Amazingly, the cardiovascular system is the first to function in an embryo. At week five, the beating heart, about the size of a poppy seed, can be seen on an ultrasound screen. The cardiovascular system is a bioengineering marvel. In an adult, the heart beats roughly 100,000 times a day, pumping 2,000 gallons of blood through over 60,000 miles of blood vessels.

Each year the American Red Cross conducts over 200,000 blood drives, collecting blood from more than nine million people. Did you know that one pint of blood can save up to three lives? Every two seconds someone needs a blood transfusion. Five million patients in the United States need blood every year.[35]

Blood is absolutely essential for physical life.

Blood is a liquid tissue made up of two components: plasma and cells. Plasma is the liquid portion of blood, containing mostly water (92 percent) and plasma proteins. The cellular component of blood includes three major types of cells—red blood cells, white blood cells, and platelets.

Blood provides the necessary requirements for life, and blood also protects our lives.

Cells need water, nutrients, and oxygen—and all three of these are supplied by blood. Red blood cells transport oxygen and help transport carbon dioxide. Plasma contains life-giving nutrients (e.g., glucose, fatty acids, amino acids, and vitamins) and hormones that are transported throughout the body. Plasma also contains salts and proteins that carry out a variety of critical physiological functions (including pH buffering, regulating membrane permeability, lipid transport, and blood clotting) and removes waste products from the body's cells. Every cell in the body is dependent on blood for survival.

Each day your body encounters foreign invaders that have the potential of causing harm, sickness, disease, and possibly even death. Blood carries cells that heal wounds and protect the body from infectious organisms. White blood cells provide defense and immunity as part of the body's immune response system (e.g., they clear bacteria from the body and produce antibodies to eliminate infectious organisms), and platelets are involved in the formation of blood clots to control bleeding.

From Biology to Theology

The concept that blood sustains life is largely associated with the discovery of blood circulation by William Harvey in 1616.[36] However, long before the scientific discoveries that blood was vital to physical life, the Bible declared that life was in the blood.

Cain's murder of Abel is discussed in terms of his brother's blood being shed (Genesis 4:10-11). Do you recall when God emphasized the sanctity of human life, requiring that "whoever sheds man's blood, by man his blood shall be shed" (Genesis 9:6)? And numerous other Scriptures explicitly define that the life of the flesh is in the blood (Genesis 9:4; Leviticus 17:11, 14; Deuteronomy 12:23).

Throughout the Bible, we see that blood offers the necessary provision for life and protects our lives, not just physically, but also spiritually.

Throughout the Bible, we see that blood offers the necessary provision for life and protects our lives, not just physically, but also spiritually. When Adam and Eve sinned, both physical and spiritual death entered the world. They were separated from their holy

Creator. But God sought to immediately restore the relationship. This required a blood sacrifice because "without the shedding of blood there is no remission of sin" (Hebrews 9:22). The animal sacrifice allowed for blood to be shed and also for clothing to cover Adam and Eve, providing atonement for their sin and bringing reconciliation to the relationship (Genesis 3:21).

The sacrificial system became the means for the people of God to atone for their sin and to appease the wrath of God (Genesis 8:20-22; Exodus 30:10; Leviticus 16:18, 27; 17:11; 2 Chronicles 29:24). Do you remember a situation in which blood offered protection of life? The blood of a lamb put on the doorposts protected those inside as God passed over in judgment (Exodus 12:7, 13, 22, 23; Hebrews 11:28). This miraculous event, called Passover, is still celebrated today.

We are all spiritually dead in our sin and separated from a holy God (Romans 5:10; Ephesians 2:1, 5; Colossians 2:13; Isaiah 59:2). The penalty for sin is death—physical death and, ultimately, spiritual separation from God eternally in the lake of fire (Revelation 20:14-15). Atonement of sin requires the sacrificial shedding of innocent blood. The life of a sinless substitute is offered instead of the guilty sinner. The animal sacrifices of the old covenant were preparation for and pointed to the new covenant—the final sacrifice of Jesus, since the blood of bulls and goats could not truly take away sin (Jeremiah 31:31-34; Mark 14:24; Luke 22:20; Hebrews 9:11-28, 10:1-18, 12:2).

God Himself, the Lord Jesus Christ, came down from heaven to be the sinless substitute. Jesus came to be the Lamb of God who takes away the sin of the world (John 1:29). He died in our place, paying our penalty on the cross by shedding His blood to cleanse us from all sin (John 3, 6; 1 John 1:7). Only Jesus' blood could take away our sin. Only Jesus can give life, eternal life, to the spiritually dead (John 3:16, 11:25, 14:6). This is why death in a perfect creation before sin is contrary to the gospel message.

If there was animal death before the fall of man, then God and all those who followed His pattern did useless acts. One must observe that in the atonement the animal loses its life in the place of the human. If animal death existed before the fall, then the object lesson represented by the atoning sacrifice is in reality a cruel joke.

If death is not the penalty for sin, then Christianity is meaningless. The death of Christ was made necessary because of man's sin. Man's sin brought death, which in turn brought God's Son to pay the penalty in our place.[37]

Blood is essential for physical life, but blood is also a symbol of spiritual life. Blood is amazingly complex, showing intricate design characteristics that point to our Creator. But even more amazing, our Creator's blood provides us a Savior. The shed blood of Jesus on the cross provides protection of life, appeasing and satisfying the wrath of God that we deserve because of our sin (propitiation) (Romans 3:25).

Blood is amazingly complex, showing intricate design characteristics that point to our Creator. But even more amazing, our Creator's blood provides us a Savior.

Through His blood, there is also provision for life, offering forgiveness of our sin (atonement), a restored relationship with God, and eternal life. Jesus our Creator died to be our Savior, shedding His blood to provide redemption, reconciliation, and justification (Matthew 26:28; Romans 3:25, 5:9; Ephesians 1:7, 2:12; Colossians 1:14, 20; 1 John 1:7; Revelation 1:5, 5:9, 19:13). In Christ Jesus, we are new creatures, born from above and transferred from death to life—eternal life (John 3:3, 5:24; 2 Corinthians 5:17). The giver of physical life is the giver of spiritual life.

CHAPTER

THE COST OF COMPROMISE

Now this I say lest anyone should deceive you with persuasive words. Beware lest anyone cheat you through philosophy and empty deceit, according to the tradition of men, according to the basic principles of the world, and not according to Christ. (Colossians 2:4, 8)

The biblical account of creation and the evolutionary approach to science proclaim mutually exclusive worldviews regarding biological origins. Did God create the astounding diversity and variation displayed in creation, or did creatures just happen through natural processes traceable to a common ancestor? Are we made in the image of God as a unique creation, or are we simply the latest biological progression from apes? Are mutations genetic decay instituted as part of the Curse, or are they a beneficial process required for biological development? Is death the punishment for sin or a creative force necessary to advance the species? Are ethnicities explained by God's judgment on mankind at Babel, or are they a chance product of random mutations?

Evolutionists believe millions of years of death eliminated the weak and preserved the fittest through the struggle for survival. The theory asserts that the natural selection process purges the less fit, but elimination of the individual is for the benefit of the population as a whole.[38] From the naturalists' perspective, death is a creative force in evolutionary development.

But could a world in chaos, characterized by death, be called a "very good" creation by God? Could ages of struggle and death be the creative force God used in creation, even though the Bible calls death the last *enemy* that Jesus Christ will come to conquer (1 Corinthians 15:26)?

Thus, evolution is a worldview that at its core rejects God, discredits the Bible, and disregards the gospel message.

Darwinian evolution, the backbone of the evolutionary worldview, is touted as scientific truth in describing biological origins. However, Darwin's theory of evolution was devised as a naturalistic mechanism to explain our origins apart from God. Thus, evolution is a worldview that at its core rejects God, discredits the Bible, and disregards the gospel message.

Conflicting Compromise

Many who "trust" science and believe in God are torn between the biblical account and evolutionary science. This has led to the integration of evolutionary science claims into the pages of the Genesis account. Attempting to reconcile evolutionary science with the Word of God in Genesis has resulted in a theistic evolution position that upholds the existence of God while affirming the "truths" of evolutionary science.[39] Proponents of theistic evolution contend that God simply created through the processes proposed by Darwin. They say that Darwinian evolution is the means and mechanism by which God created. Today, the *theory* of evolution has become a *theology* of evolution.[40] But given evolutionary science's anti-Christian roots, is theistic evolution a viable doctrine of creation, or is it an imposter proposing a conflicting compromise?

God's Nature Compromised

What is often lacking in this debate is an evaluation of the nature of God. The Bible says that creation reveals the nature of God (Romans 1:20, Psalm 19:1-3). Therefore, God must have created according to His own nature and character.

Although God is all-powerful and all-knowing, could God have created through evolutionary processes (e.g., Big Bang and Darwinian evolution)? Could God have created using whatever method He so desired?

Actually, God is limited by His own nature, meaning that "God can do anything that is an absolute possibility *and not inconsistent with any of his basic attributes.*"[41]

Given these "limitations" based on God's nature, is theistic evolution a philosophical and theological possibility? Evolutionary processes are characterized by chaos, chance, confusion, destruction, struggle, and pain. For organisms to have developed through evolutionary processes, millions of years of suffering and death are necessary. Are the chaos, confusion, and other characteristics associated with evolutionary processes consistent with the nature and character of God?

God's creation must show purpose, a plan, design, and order. He is not the author of randomness or confusion, and He can only do perfect works.

The Bible tells us that God is all-powerful, all-knowing, perfect, ordered, and holy (Isaiah 6:3, Matthew 10:29-30, Psalm 147:4, Revelation 4:8). What do these attributes of God require in relation to God's creative work? God's creation must show purpose, a plan, design, and order. He is not the author of randomness or confusion, and He can only do perfect works (1 Corinthians 14:33, Isaiah 55:11, Psalm 18:30).[42]

God is the Creator and giver of life, physically and spiritually. But evolution is predicated upon death. Could God employ mechanisms and methods that contradict His basic attributes? No! Just as God cannot lie because lying is inconsistent with His nature (e.g., holy, perfect, truth, sinless; Titus 1:2), the actions of God required by theistic evolution are incompatible and inconsistent with the nature of God. The processes of evolution are mutually exclusive to the characteristics of God's nature.

God's Word Compromised

Reinterpreting Genesis in light of evolutionary science has begun a domino effect of theological compromises that impact many foundational doctrines of Christianity. For instance, if humanity developed through chance random mutations and natural selection, how do we explain a literal and historical Adam and Eve? Elevating evolutionary science over Scripture has led to the belief that a historical and literal Adam and Eve do not fit the scientific evidence. This, then, has naturally progressed to a rejection of the Fall and the life and death of Jesus as our redemptive sacrifice.

Today we are seeing the significant cost of compromise as evolutionary science defines doctrine and becomes the decisive factor in the interpretation of Scripture. The point of contention is no longer just origins. Many of the doctrines of Christianity (e.g., the historicity of Adam, the Fall, the global Flood, and the redemption of Jesus) are being reinterpreted due to the elevation of evolutionary science as truth, and the authoritative truth of God's Word is being rejected.

The Gospel Message Compromised

Accepting the origins of humanity based upon evolutionary science causes many to question the validity of the biblical message of Christ's redemptive work. If biological death always existed and was the means for creating new forms of life—including us—how is there meaning in Christ's death for our sin?

Theistic evolution's claim that millions of years of death existed before humanity and before sin corrupts the biblical narrative. The Bible emphatically states that death entered God's perfect creation due to the sin of Adam (Genesis 3, Romans 5:12-21, 1 Corinthians 15:20-26). Death is the penalty for sin, necessitating our need for a Savior to provide the forgiveness of sin and eternal life (Romans 5:12, 6:23).

Death before the Fall cannot be reconciled with the gospel message. If death existed before sin, death cannot be the penalty for sin. If death preceded sin, the animal sacrifices could not have been the payment for sin. If death existed before sin, then the death of Jesus on the cross cannot be the judgment for sin. Death is necessary for redemption; the Creator must die to bring life.

If death existed before sin, death cannot be the penalty for sin.

Is this just an insignificant theological debate? Consider the comments by an atheist related to these issues:

Christianity has fought, still fights, and will continue to fight science to the desperate end over evolution, because evolution destroys utterly and finally the very reason Jesus' earthly life was supposedly made necessary. Destroy Adam and Eve and the original sin, and in the rubble you will find the sorry remains of the Son of God. If Jesus was not the redeemer who died for our sins, and this is what evolution means, then Christianity is nothing.[43]

Is death the judgment for sin (a result of the Curse and Fall) or a necessary creative process used by God? Theistic evolution makes God the author of evil and death.[44] Evolution contends, "By struggle, suffering, and death came man! But this directly contradicts the biblical revelation: 'By man came death...' (1 Corinthians 15:21)."[45] This is why we need the Savior that God so graciously sent to heal our suffering and to conquer death (1 Corinthians 15:16, Revelation 21:4-5).

Conclusion

Many today adamantly seek to integrate evolutionary science into the creation account of Genesis, claiming that God created through evolutionary processes. The proposition of theistic evolution compromises God's nature, God's Word, and the gospel message, resulting in the rejection of many doctrines foundational to Christianity. The battle of authority between God's Word and evolutionary science is not an insignificant theological debate. Many today are rejecting Christianity because of the apparent discrepancy between the Bible and science, citing that they cannot trust the Bible since Genesis is at odds with the evolutionary science that they believe is authoritative truth.[46]

So which *did* come first—the chicken or the egg? The Bible is clear that just as God created all the animals fully functional in the beginning, the chicken came first. By going to Scripture, you can answer more of the tough questions posed by those who are confused by the claims of evolution proponents.

The God of life has given us clear answers to the questions of life, including biological origins, in His inerrant, infallible Word. The biblical account provides the most rational answers to the questions of life and continues to be upheld by new scientific discoveries. We can have confidence in the authoritative truth of God's Word. As Creator, God alone defines biology and the source of truth to answer the questions of biological origins.

NOTES

1. Tomkins, J. P. 2012. *The Design and Complexity of the Cell*. Dallas, TX: Institute for Creation Research, 15-17.
2. Morris, H. M. and H. M. Morris III. 1996. *Many Infallible Proofs*. Green Forest, AR: Master Books, 270-71.
3. Batten, D. 2000. Ligers and wholphins? What next? *Creation*. 22 (3): 28-33.
4. Jeanson, N. 2011. Molecular Equidistance: The Echo of Discontinuity? *Acts & Facts*. 40 (2): 6.
5. Sweetlove, L. Number of species on Earth tagged at 8.7 million. *Nature News*. Posted on nature.com August 23, 2011.
6. Snelling, A. A. 2009. *Earth's Catastrophic Past*, Vol. 1. Dallas, TX: Institute for Creation Research, 137.
7. Thomas, B. Study Shows Bird Species Change Fast. *ICR News*. Posted on icr.org December 21, 2011; Morris, H. 1984. *The Biblical Basis for Modern Science*. Grand Rapids, MI: Baker, 350-51.
8. Criswell, D. 2009. Speciation and the Animals on the Ark. *Acts & Facts*. 38 (4): 10.
9. Parker, G. and J. Tomkins. 2010. *Genetic Diversity*. Dallas, TX: Institute for Creation Research; Tomkins, J. 2012. Mechanisms of Adaptation in Biology: Genetic Diversity. *Acts & Facts*. 41 (5): 8; Tomkins, J. Gene Control Regions Are Protected—Negating Evolution. *ICR News*. Posted on icr.org June 11, 2012.
10. Parker and Tomkins, *Genetic Diversity*.
11. Guliuzza, R. J. 2009. *Made in His Image: Examining the Complexities of the Human Body*. Dallas, TX: Institute for Creation Research, 20.
12. Bergman, J. 1984. Mankind—The Pinnacle of God's Creation. *Acts & Facts*. 13 (7).
13. Behe, M. 1996. *Darwin's Black Box*. New York, NY: Simon and Schuster, 39.
14. Thomas, B. Are Humans as Close to Chickens as They Are to Chimps? *ICR News*. Posted on icr.org January 26, 2010; Tompkins, J. 2012. Human-Chimp DNA Comparison Research Yields Lower Genetic Similarity. *Acts & Facts*. 41 (1): 8; Jeanson, N. and J. Tomkins. 2011. Human-Chimp Genetic Similarity: Is the Evolutionary Dogma Valid? *Acts & Facts*. 40 (7): 6; Tomkins, J. 2011. Evaluating the Human-Chimp DNA Myth—New Research Data. *Acts & Facts*. 40 (10): 6; Thomas, B. DNA Study Contradicts Human/Chimp Common Ancestry. *ICR News*. Posted on icr.org November 15, 2011.
15. Tomkins, J. 2009. Human-Chimp Similarities: Common Ancestry or Flawed Research? *Acts & Facts*. 38 (6): 12.
16. The Joshua Project. Posted on joshuaproject.net.
17. Morris, H. Origin of the Races. *Days of Praise*, April 14, 1993; Morris, H. 1973. Evolution and Modern Racism. *Acts & Facts*. 2 (7).
18. Morris, J. 1997. Did the African Eve Leave Footprints? *Acts & Facts*. 26 (10).
19. Morris, H. 1975. Language, Creation and the Inner Man. *Acts & Facts*. 4 (8).
20. Carter, R. W. The Non-Mythical Adam and Eve!: Refuting errors by Francis Collins and BioLogos. Creation Ministries International. Posted on creation.com August 20, 2011; Thomas, B. Christian Professor Claims Genetics Disproves Historical Adam. *ICR News*. Posted on icr.org August 26, 2011.
21. Parker, G. 1980. Creation, Mutation, and Variation. *Acts & Facts*. 9 (11).
22. Thomas, B. Neandertal Genome Confirms Creation Science Predictions. *ICR News*. Posted on icr.org May 28, 2010; Thomas, B. Neandertals Mixed with Humans in China. *ICR News*. Posted on icr.org November 3, 2010.
23. Wood, T. C. 2001. Genome Decay in the Mycoplasmas. *Acts & Facts*. 30 (10).
24. Morris, J. 2005. How Did Noah Gather the Animals? *Acts & Facts*. 34 (9).
25. Wood, Genome Decay in the Mycoplasmas.
26. Thomas, B. Is There a Stuttering Gene? *ICR News*. Posted on icr.org February 26, 2010.
27. Parker, Creation, Mutation, and Variation.
28. Sherwin, F. 2004. Mending Mistakes—The Amazing Ability of Repair. *Acts & Facts*. 33 (6).
29. Thomas, B. Antibiotic Resistance in Bacteria Did Not Evolve. *ICR News*. Posted on icr.org May 10, 2011; Thomas, B. 2011. Antibiotic Resistance in Bacteria Shows Adaptive Design. *Acts & Facts*. 40 (7): 18; Stephens, J. C. et al. 1998. Dating the Origin of the $CCR5-\Delta32$ AIDS-Resistance Allele by the Coalescence of Haplotypes. *American Journal of Human Genetics*. 62 (6): 1507-1515.
30. Chial, H. 2008. Mendelian genetics: Patterns of inheritance and single-gene disorders. *Nature Education*. 1 (1).
31. Morris III, H. 2009. *The Big Three: Major Events that Changed History Forever*. Green Forest, AR: Master Books, 161.
32. Morris, *The Biblical Basis for Modern Science*, 219.
33. Morris, J. 1991. Are Plants Alive? *Acts & Facts*. 20: (9).
34. MacArthur, J. 2001. *The Battle for the Beginning*. Nashville, TN: Thomas Nelson, 195.
35. Learn About Blood. American Red Cross fact sheet. Posted on redcrossblood.org.
36. Morris, *The Biblical Basis for Modern Science*, 346.
37. Stambaugh, J. 1989. Death before Sin? *Acts & Facts*. 18 (5).
38. Colling, R. G. 2004. *Random Design: Created from Chaos to Connect with the Creator*. Bourbonnais, IL: Browning Press, 77.
39. Swarbrick, M. W. 2006. *Theistic Evolution: Did God Create Through Evolution?* West Conshohocken, PA: Infinity Publishing, 12-13.
40. Jackelen, A. 2007. A Critical View of Theistic Evolution. *Theology and Science*. 5 (2): 151.
41. Rowe, W. L. 2007. *Philosophy of Religion*. Belmont, CA: Wadsworth, 7-8.
42. Morris III, H. 2003. *After Eden*. Green Forest, AR: Master Books, 119-121.
43. Stambaugh, Death Before Sin?
44. Morris, *After Eden*, 42.
45. Morris, H. 2005. *The Long War Against God*. Green Forest, AR: Master Books, 113.
46. Ham, K. and B. Beemer. 2011. *Already Gone*. Green Forest, AR: Master Books, 95-116.

ABOUT THE AUTHOR

DR. BRAD FORLOW received his B.S. in Chemical Engineering at Florida Institute of Technology, and his Ph.D. in Chemical Engineering at the University of Oklahoma. For four years he held the post of Assistant Professor of Research at the University of Virginia before working in pharmaceutical research for an additional six years, most recently for Wyeth/Pfizer. In addition to his science training, Dr. Forlow earned an M.Div. at Southwestern Baptist Theological Seminary. Dr. Forlow currently serves on the life science research team at the Institute for Creation Research in Dallas, Texas, as well as functioning as Associate Science Editor at the Institute. He is married to Dr. Rhonda Forlow, who serves as ICR's K-12 Education Specialist. Brad Forlow's books include *Five Evidences for a Global Flood* and *7 Creation Miracles of Christ*. The Forlows have three children and reside in Dallas.

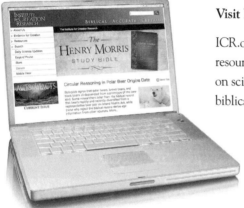